Conquering SAD
(Seasonal Affective Disorder)

A Comprehensive Guide to Overcoming Seasonal Affective Disorder and Embracing All Seasons with Ease

Isabella White

Copyright © 2023 by Isabella White.

The publisher reserves all rights. Without prior written permission, no part of this publication may be reproduced, distributed, or transmitted in any form or by any means, including photocopying, recording, or other electronic or mechanical methods. Under copyright law, limited quotations may be used for non-commercial purposes and critical reviews.

__Disclaimer:__ The information in this book is based on the author's research, opinions, and experiences. It is not intended to replace professional medical advice or treatment. The reader should regularly consult a physician for any health issues and always seek the advice of a physician before modifying diet, supplement, or exercise regimens. The author and publisher shall have neither liability nor responsibility to any person or entity concerning any loss or damage related to the information contained in this book. The information provided is general and may not apply to every individual. Any reliance on the information contained herein is solely at the reader's risk.

Table of Contents

Chapter 7
Making Your Environment SAD-Proof_______ 70

Conclusion_________________________________ 80

Introduction

The first time I felt it was on a cold, gray day in November. I was driving to work, looking at the bare trees and leaden sky, when an unshakeable sadness settled over me. I sighed, realizing the long winter months were ahead.

By January, I dreaded getting out of bed in the morning. I lacked motivation, skipping my usual workout routine. At work, I struggled to concentrate, making careless mistakes. My appetite increased, and I craved sugary, starchy comfort foods. I felt terrible. The worst part was feeling hopeless and worthless. My mind was constantly bombarded with negative thoughts that I could not shake off.

My sleep schedule shifted later and later, making mornings bleak and challenging. I isolated myself from friends and family, avoiding social activities I once enjoyed. When the weekends came, I stayed huddled under the blankets rather than going outside. The winter days blurred together in an endless slog of darkness.

It was not until March that I realized something was wrong. I googled my symptoms and learned about seasonal affective disorder. Suddenly, it all made sense—the lethargy, depression, oversleeping, overeating, and social withdrawal I experienced every winter. I was not just having a bad few months; I had a recognized condition triggered by the change of seasons.

With this new understanding, I committed to properly treating my SAD. I tried light therapy, forcing myself to sit before a sunlight-simulating lamp every morning. I also started taking vitamin D supplements to compensate for the lack of sun exposure. Establishing a regular exercise routine boosted my mood through those long, cold months.

While my SAD never fully went away, these interventions helped me better manage it year after year. The seasons continued to change, but I changed, too, learning how to embrace the distinct beauty of each one. I discovered ways to thrive in the winter that previously burdened me. My story illustrates that SAD can be conquered with knowledge, commitment, and the right strategies.

Statistics on the Prevalence of SAD

Seasonal Affective Disorder is a surprisingly common condition that impacts millions of people each year. Estimates show that it affects 10–20% of the population in the United States. The reported rates are even higher in some countries, like Canada, where prevalence is estimated at 15–30%.

Women are diagnosed with SAD at about four times the rate of men. Some research indicates that females may have increased vulnerability due to hormonal fluctuations related to their menstrual cycles and shifts in circadian rhythms.

SAD is more frequently diagnosed in younger individuals, with the average age of onset being in the early 20s. However, it can impact people of any age. The disorder also tends to be more prevalent the farther people live from the equator. Individuals in northern latitudes with long, severe winters and short daylight hours face increased risk.

Around 1-2% of the U.S. population experiences winter-pattern SAD, which follows a yearly pattern with symptoms emerging in late fall or winter and subsiding in spring. An estimated 10–20% likely have a milder form called Subsyndromal Seasonal Affective Disorder with less intense symptoms that still impair functioning.

Only about 1–2% of the population has summer-pattern SAD, with depressive episodes manifesting in spring and summer. This form of the disorder is rare and not as thoroughly researched. However, its prevalence also illustrates that SAD can happen any time of year, not just in the winter.

Finally, an estimated 20–30% of SAD patients have symptoms all year, to varying degrees. While they may still experience worsening in certain seasons, their condition is not limited to a specific time of year. This demonstrates how SAD exists on a spectrum, with some people having very seasonal fluctuations while others struggle more consistently.

Overall, the takeaway is that SAD is an extensively prevalent condition affecting millions worldwide. However, it remains underdiagnosed and undertreated in many cases. Increased awareness and understanding of SAD statistics can help patients identify when they may benefit from intervention strategies. Knowing you are not alone is an empowering first step in taking charge of seasonal depression.

How This Book Will Help Readers Conquer Seasonal Affective Disorder

If you pick up this book, you can identify with the dread that sets in as the days grow shorter and colder. You may isolate yourself more, sleep and overeat more, and feel fatigued or depressed during the winter months. These are hallmark signs of a condition called Seasonal Affective Disorder (SAD) that impacts millions worldwide.

The good news is that SAD is treatable, and this book provides a comprehensive game plan for overcoming it. I will share the knowledge I have accumulated from researching and personally experiencing SAD. By the end, you will have a complete toolkit of strategies to conquer seasonal depression for good.

We will begin by getting a firm understanding of what SAD is and what causes it. I will provide an overview of diagnostic criteria, risk factors, and theories on the underlying mechanisms. A thorough comprehension of SAD sets the stage for developing customized management techniques.

Next, we will go through step-by-step, evidence-based treatment options, like light therapy, medications, psychotherapy, and lifestyle changes. I will share actionable advice on how to build an effective regimen tailored to your needs and symptoms. You will learn how to adapt these tools during different seasons.

Since diet, exercise, sleep, and routines play a huge role in SAD, we will devote focused sections to mastering each domain. I will provide guidance on nutrition, fitness regimens, sleep hygiene, morning and evening rituals, scheduling, and more. Implementing healthy habits in these areas can work wonders.

We will also discuss how to tweak your mindset and cope with the emotional challenges of SAD. You will learn cognitive strategies, mindfulness practices, and ways to manage stress and negative thoughts. Boosting mental well-being goes hand-in-hand with physical interventions.

Additionally, I will offer tips on preparing your environment, like maximizing light exposure and color palettes. Simple adjustments to your home and workspace can make a difference. We will also discuss seasonal wardrobe changes, travel, social connections, and outdoor activities.

Applying this book's holistic set of solutions allows you to take charge of your SAD and thrive year-round. I aim to share the key insights and tools I wish I had known earlier in my journey. By raising awareness and empowering readers with proven techniques, I hope that nobody has to suffer through the isolation of SAD alone. Together, we can conquer seasonal depression for good.

Chapter 1

Understanding SAD

Definition, Diagnostic Criteria, and Symptoms of SAD

Seasonal Affective Disorder (SAD) is a type of depression that emerges and subsides in correlation with seasonal changes throughout the year. The main diagnostic criteria for SAD include the following:

- Depressed mood and other symptoms of depression start in the fall or winter months and improve in the spring. The symptoms must have occurred for at least two consecutive years.

- These depressive episodes must outnumber any non-seasonal depressive episodes the individual experiences over their lifetime.
- The seasonal depressive symptoms must be more extreme than any fluctuations experienced outside of that time.
- Other disorders, such as bipolar or schizoaffective disorder, do not explain depression any better.
- The symptoms cause significant distress or impairment in daily functioning.

The core symptoms used to diagnose major depressive disorder can also indicate SAD if they manifest seasonally. These include:

- Depressed, sad mood for most of the day, nearly every day. Feelings of emptiness, hopelessness, irritability, guilt, and worthlessness.
- Markedly diminished interest in activities once enjoyed—loss of motivation and drive.
- Significant weight loss when not dieting, or weight gain and increased appetite.
- Difficulty sleeping (insomnia) or sleeping excessively.

- Physical and mental fatigue; slowness in movement and thought.
- Restlessness and agitation.
- Lack of focus and concentration, indecisiveness.
- Thoughts of death, suicide, or suicide attempts.

Additional symptoms commonly associated with the winter pattern of SAD include:

- Oversleeping and daytime drowsiness
- Carbohydrate cravings and overeating
- Social withdrawal, loss of interest in social activities
- Loss of libido
- Physical hypersensitivity to cold and an exaggerated response to dropping temperatures

The spring and summer SAD pattern tends to manifest with symptoms like:

- Trouble sleeping and insomnia
- Poor appetite, weight loss
- Agitation, anxiety, and restlessness
- Violent thoughts and behavior

Tracking the onset and resolution of these seasonal symptoms is key to an accurate SAD diagnosis. This establishes a clear time pattern tied to the changing seasons.

The Causes and Risk Factors of SAD

While researchers are still working to unlock the precise mechanisms behind SAD, several key causes and risk factors have been identified:

Reduced Sunlight Exposure:
The most agreed-upon cause is insufficient sunlight in certain seasons, particularly winter. Sunlight helps regulate our circadian rhythms and balance brain chemicals like serotonin and melatonin that influence mood. Insufficient sunlight can disrupt this biological rhythm.

Melatonin and Serotonin Imbalances:
Closely tied to light exposure are imbalances in melatonin and serotonin, two hormones that regulate sleep, mood, and other bodily functions. Melatonin levels remain elevated in the darker months, making some people drowsy. Meanwhile, decreases in serotonin are associated with low mood and energy.

Seasonal Changes in the Circadian Rhythm:

Our circadian rhythm is a 24-hour internal body clock that regulates sleep-wake cycles and other important processes. Some research suggests this rhythm is delayed or disrupted during darker seasons, contributing to SAD symptoms.

Vitamin D Deficiency:

Vitamin D is produced when the skin is exposed to sunlight and UV rays. Low vitamin D levels are correlated with depressive symptoms, and vitamin D oral supplements may improve SAD.

Genetics and Family History:

Studies indicate that genetics play a role in SAD risk. People with first-degree relatives who have SAD or other forms of depression are at increased risk of developing seasonal depression themselves.

Female Sex:

As mentioned earlier, women are diagnosed with SAD at much higher rates than men, though the exact reasons are still debated. Reproductive hormones, brain chemistry differences, and cultural and behavioral factors may contribute.

Living Far North or South:

Proximity to the equator also impacts risk, with SAD prevalence increasing the farther north or south someone lives. Populations farther from the equator receive less sunlight during the winter months.

Age:

Younger populations have higher rates of SAD, with symptoms often appearing in early adulthood. However, people of any age can develop SAD.

Overall, light exposure, genetics, hormones, geography, age, and gender represent key factors that may cause and indicate risk for seasonal depression, though more research is still needed.

Differentiating SAD from Other Similar Conditions

The cyclic nature of seasonal affective disorder can make it easily confused with other conditions related to mood and sleep. However, recognizing the distinguishing features of SAD is vital for proper diagnosis and treatment.

Major Depressive Disorder:

While SAD is classified under the umbrella of major depressive disorder, key differences exist. The depression associated with SAD occurs during specific seasons, while major depressive disorder persists year-round. SAD also has unique symptoms like oversleeping, overeating, and carbohydrate cravings that are not requisite for a major depression diagnosis.

Bipolar Disorder:

In bipolar disorder, individuals cycle between periods of depression and mania with high energy and activity levels. SAD only involves cyclic episodes of depression, not mania. The seasons, rather than irregular mood swings, dictate depressive periods in SAD.

Chronic Fatigue Syndrome:

Chronic fatigue shares the decreased energy and exhaustion of SAD. However, it does not follow a seasonal pattern. Fatigue persists throughout the year rather than remitting in sunnier seasons. Chronic fatigue also lacks other SAD indicators, like oversleeping and overeating.

Seasonal Allergies:

Allergies can coincide with SAD seasonal timelines and share symptoms like fatigue and mood changes. However, allergies cause additional symptoms like sneezing, coughing, and irritated eyes, nose, and throat. Getting an allergy test can help determine if allergies are the culprit.

Hypothyroidism:

An underactive thyroid can mimic SAD with fatigue, weight gain, sleep issues, and depression. However, hypothyroidism symptoms are not seasonal. Checking thyroid hormone levels can determine if thyroid issues are causing or contributing to depression.

Premenstrual Dysphoric Disorder (PMDD):

PMDD triggers depressive symptoms cyclically, like SAD. However, the timing follows menstruation cycles rather than seasons. Tracking symptoms against menstrual calendars can reveal if they correlate specifically with menstrual timing.

The seasonal pattern is the hallmark differentiator for SAD diagnosis. Keeping a mood and symptom journal for at least a year can help identify if changes align with seasonal shifts versus other disorders. If symptoms do not improve in the summer months, other conditions could be explored as potential diagnoses or co-occurring illnesses.

Research on the Prevalence, Age Patterns, and Gender Differences Related to SAD

Extensive research has been conducted to estimate the prevalence of seasonal affective disorder in the general population and identify patterns related to age and gender.

Prevalence Rates:

Most studies estimate that SAD affects around 5% of the U.S. population, though rates vary by location. The prevalence rises to over 10% in northern latitudes like Alaska and New England. Rates are generally higher among European populations versus African Americans or those near the equator.

Globally, SAD prevalence ranges from 1–10% across different countries. Several Scandinavian nations report rates ranging from 8–10%. Countries like Iran and Israel document far lower SAD rates, around 1-2%, due to increased sunlight exposure.

Age Patterns:

SAD usually develops early in life, with the typical onset occurring between 18 and 30 years old. Rates tend to peak between 20 and 40 years old. One study found that 12% of adolescents experienced SAD, demonstrating that it can develop even earlier.

Later-onset SAD is less common but does occur. The precise age patterns are influenced by geography. Younger populations have higher rates in more polar locations, while SAD onset skews slightly older closer to the equator.

Gender Differences:

The most robust, replicated finding is that SAD disproportionately afflicts women over men. Approximately 75–85% of diagnosed SAD cases occur in women. This holds across geographic locations and age groups.

Some research documents women experiencing more severe impairment symptoms of SAD as well. However, a subset of studies observe similar depression severity in men and women with SAD.

Explanations for the pronounced gender discrepancy are still speculative. Women's increased vulnerability could stem from hormonal fluctuations, cultural influences, cognitive traits like rumination, biological differences in circadian rhythms or neurotransmitters, or some combination.

Contemporary research converges on SAD as a fairly prevalent disorder impacting around 5% of the general population and up to 10–20% in far northern areas, with young adults and women representing the majority of cases. However, SAD can impact people of any demographic. Continuing to advance our understanding of who is most impacted can help target prevention and treatment.

Chapter 2

The Physical Impact of SAD

How Light Deficiency Impacts Circadian Rhythms

The circadian rhythm is our internal biological clock that regulates sleep-wake cycles and other important bodily processes over 24 hours. Exposure to natural daylight plays a critical role in setting and maintaining this rhythm. When daylight hours shorten in the winter, it can throw off our circadian cycles and cause the physical symptoms of Seasonal Affective Disorder (SAD).

Research shows that the circadian rhythms of people with SAD are often delayed or shifted compared to normal cycles. The rhythm needs to reset itself properly in the absence of adequate sunlight exposure early in the day.

This circadian mismatch is what causes many SAD sufferers to experience fatigue and oversleeping in the mornings since their internal clock is shifted later. It also contributes to difficulty falling asleep at an appropriate bedtime, leading to tossing and turning through the night.

The circadian disruption also reduces the production of essential hormones like cortisol and melatonin. Cortisol helps regulate energy and alertness levels throughout the day. Reduced sunlight can diminish cortisol release in the mornings, making it hard to feel awake and focused early in the day.

Melatonin is the sleep-regulating hormone that rises in the evenings to induce drowsiness. Insufficient sunlight exposure inhibits the suppression of melatonin levels in the morning. This leads to carryover drowsiness and brain fog through the daytime hours.

Out-of-sync circadian rhythms underlie the constant drowsiness, low motivation, and desire to sleep more characterize SAD. Light is the primary external cue that keeps our internal body clock aligned, throwing the whole system off balance if it is lacking.

Downstream, the circadian disruption also negatively impacts digestion, blood pressure regulation, body temperature, immune system function, and key metabolic processes. Every cell in the body follows circadian cycles, so misalignments create systemic dysfunction.

Overall, daylight savings plays a pivotal role in regulating our circadian rhythms and keeping the time-sensitive biological processes of our bodies on track. When we do not get sufficient daytime light exposure, especially in the mornings, our internal cycles get pushed later and later. This leads to the feeling of "winter time jetlag" and the low energy, disrupted sleep patterns, and overall physical malaise that plague SAD sufferers through the darker months.

The Roles of Serotonin, Melatonin, and Other Hormones

Imbalances and dysregulation in key neurotransmitters and hormones appear to contribute to the physiological and psychological symptoms of SAD. Let us explore the roles of serotonin, melatonin, cortisol, vitamin D, and endorphins.

Serotonin:

Low serotonin levels are strongly linked to symptoms of depression and also fluctuate with seasonal changes. Sunlight exposure boosts serotonin synthesis, so the decrease in daylight hours during the winter limits serotonin production. These shortages can lead to a depressed mood, low energy, a lack of motivation, and other SAD symptoms.

Melatonin:

Melatonin regulates sleep by rising in the evening to induce drowsiness and declining in the morning to promote alertness. Melatonin remains elevated with the longer nights of winter, making people feel sleepier. Light exposure in the morning is meant to inhibit melatonin, so insufficient daylight prevents melatonin from dropping to wake people up properly.

Cortisol:

This important hormone peaks in the morning to increase energy and then declines to facilitate sleep. However, the circadian dips and spikes in cortisol can become irregular with seasonal changes, especially with less sunlight in the winter. Abnormal cortisol rhythms lead to fatigue, daytime sleepiness, and other SAD symptoms.

Vitamin D:

Sometimes called the "sunshine vitamin," vitamin D is produced in the body through exposure to natural sunlight. Less daylight in winter means reduced vitamin D, which may contribute to seasonal depression. Low vitamin D is linked to low mood and fatigue. Supplements can compensate for the winter shortfalls in sunlight-derived vitamin D.

Endorphins:

Physical activity typically triggers the release of endorphins, the body's "feel-good" chemicals that boost mood and relieve stress. However, the lethargy and lack of motivation associated with SAD lead to reduced physical activity. In turn, endorphin levels decline, perpetuating a depressed mood. Making exercise a priority counteracts this.

Overall, SAD involves complex interactions between natural light exposure and the body's intricate hormone and neurotransmitter activity, regulating mood, sleep, energy, and more. Strategically timing light exposure, physical activity, and vitamin D supplementation can help compensate for wintertime hormonal changes and rebalance the system. Paying attention to our biological rhythms provides clues for overcoming SAD.

Why some people are biologically prone to SAD

The precise reasons why certain individuals are more vulnerable to SAD from a biological standpoint remain unclear. However, research points to several influential factors:

Genetics:

Genetic predisposition plays a significant role. People with a first-degree relative—parents, siblings, or children—diagnosed with SAD are at increased risk. Twin studies reveal that monozygotic twins show higher concordance rates for SAD than dizygotic twins, implicating inherited genetics. Specific gene variants involved in serotonin regulation and circadian rhythms have been tentatively linked to SAD risk.

Sex Hormones:

As previously discussed, women have much higher rates of SAD, pointing to sex hormones as a potential contributor. Estrogen and progesterone fluctuate with women's menstrual cycles, which could make them more sensitive to seasonal light changes. The declines in estrogen and progesterone during menopause may trigger SAD onset in some middle-aged women.

Brain Chemistry:

People with SAD seem prone to anomalies in brain circuits and neurotransmitters that regulate sleep, mood, appetite, and cognition. Imbalances in serotonin, dopamine, and melatonin could stem from underlying brain chemistry and circuitry differences. Light therapy works by normalizing activity in these mood-regulating brain networks.

Circadian Rhythms:

Variations in circadian clock genes and misalignments between internal rhythms and external cycles of light and dark have been implicated in SAD. Circadian disruptions like delayed sleep phases are more common in individuals with seasonal depression. Their clocks struggle to adapt normally to seasonal light changes.

Retinal Circuitry:

Differences in the retina and visual systems of those vulnerable to SAD affect how their eyes, brains, and biological clocks respond to light exposure. Their internal cycles may require brighter light in the mornings and darkness at night to properly entrain. Deficits in cells that help synchronize to light have been proposed.

Overall, while more research is still needed, it appears that an intricate interplay of genetic predispositions, sex hormone fluctuations, brain and retinal circuitry intricacies, and circadian rhythms that are more easily disrupted likely converge to create a "perfect storm," rendering certain individuals more susceptible to Seasonal Affective Disorder and its symptoms. Unlocking the biological underpinnings paves the way for better treatment and prevention approaches.

The Toll SAD Takes on Physical Health

In addition to the psychological impact, the physiological changes associated with SAD can take a toll on overall physical health and well-being. Some of the key effects include:

Weight Gain:
Overeating and cravings for carbohydrate-rich foods lead many SAD sufferers to gain weight, particularly through the winter months. This weight gain then exacerbates the feelings of sluggishness and low energy characteristic of SAD.

Cardiovascular Effects:

Studies link SAD to adverse impacts on heart health. Seasonal depressive symptoms show spikes in inflammatory heart disease markers. They have increased blood pressure and restricted blood flow during the winter months—key risk factors for cardiovascular disease over time.

Metabolic Disruption:

Thyroid issues and metabolic syndrome become more common in people with SAD. The thyroid regulates metabolism, so its disruption contributes to fatigue and weight gain. Blood sugar and insulin irregularities also occur. These metabolic changes increase diabetes risk.

Weakened Immunity:

SAD has been associated with impairments in immune system function. Inflammatory markers rise to higher levels during the winter months. People produce fewer antibodies in response to flu vaccines when they are susceptible to SAD. Wintertime colds and cases of flu hit them harder.

Musculoskeletal Pain:

The slump in activity levels and poor mood frequently lead to increased musculoskeletal discomfort and pain sensitivity in winter. Backaches, stiff necks, joint pain, and headaches worsen. The winter blues make your whole body hurt more.

Cognitive Impairment:

SAD patients exhibit deficits in reaction times, information processing, attention, and memory, specifically during their seasonal depressive episodes. The brain fog of SAD takes a toll on cognitive performance, impairing productivity.

The wide-ranging physiological shifts underlying SAD—from metabolic changes to immune dysfunction to musculoskeletal issues—impact overall physical well-being. Adopting nutrition, exercise, sleep, and light therapy practices to counteract SAD can mitigate these detrimental effects. Remaining vigilant about physical health helps avoid long-term damage.

Chapter 3

The Emotional Effects of SAD

The Links Between SAD and Depression and Anxiety Symptoms

The core psychological impact of SAD is the onset of major depressive symptoms in correlation with seasonal changes. These include:

- Depressed, sad mood and frequent crying spells
- Loss of interest in and pleasure in normally enjoyable activities
- Fatigue, lack of energy, and motivation
- Feelings of hopelessness, worthlessness, and guilt
- Difficulty concentrating and making decisions

- Sleep disturbances - insomnia or hypersomnia
- Appetite changes - overeating, cravings for carbs
- Suicidal thoughts in severe cases

SAD can also coincide with symptoms of anxiety and anxious distress:

- Feeling tense, "on edge," restless, or panic attacks
- Increased worries about future or past events
- Social anxiety and avoiding social situations
- Obsessions, compulsions, and repetitive thoughts
- Irritability, agitation

Some research shows powerful links between SAD and:

1. **Social anxiety:** Many people with SAD withdraw from social activities and avoid crowds during depressive episodes.
2. **Panic attacks:** Feelings of panic may arise from the lack of sunlight and the increase in gloomy weather during winter slumps.
3. **Agoraphobia:** In severe cases, some SAD sufferers become afraid of leaving their homes and entering public spaces.

4. **Generalized anxiety:** Rumination increases for those with SAD as they obsessively focus on their winter depression.

SAD involves dealing with the difficult emotional turbulence of depression annually as the seasons change. Low mood, despair, disinterest, low energy, and isolation all take their toll. High anxiety often accompanies the condition, too. However, recognizing these links to mood disorders empowers sufferers to be proactive and utilize proven treatments.

Lack of Motivation, Isolation, and Loneliness Experienced in the Winter

As the days grow shorter and colder, many people with SAD notice their motivation and interest in social activities plummeting. They start withdrawing into isolation and experience profound loneliness during the winter months. Several factors contribute to this:

Lack of Motivation:

Reducing natural sunlight exposure decreases serotonin levels and disrupts circadian rhythms that influence our energy levels. This physiological change creates a sense of lethargy and difficulty getting motivated to complete tasks or engage in hobbies. Even enjoyable activities feel like too much effort.

Avoidance of Outdoors:

Some outrightly avoid going outside as temperatures drop. The cold and gloomy weather makes the outdoors unappealing. Shorter days provide less opportunity to get outside. Instead, they want to stay indoors, away from the dreary winter landscape.

Discomfort in Public Spaces:

Crowded public spaces like shopping malls, stadiums, and holiday markets induce stress for SAD sufferers when depressed. Sensory overload from lights, noise, and crowds overwhelms them, causing them to avoid leaving the house.

Canceling Plans and Commitments:

As energy levels sink and the desire for human interaction wanes, individuals with SAD start declining social invitations and canceling plans with friends and family. They turn down parties, sporting events, and other activities they would otherwise enjoy during the warmer months.

Preferring Solitude:

In the depths of a seasonal depressive episode, solitude often feels more comforting than social stimulation. Being around other people becomes tedious and draining. Withdrawing into isolation can feel like the only way to relieve the sadness.

Increased Screen Time:
Without work or social commitments motivating them to leave the house, people with SAD easily fall into the habit of staying glued to electronic devices all day long. They binge-watch TV and doomscroll social media in the absence of human interaction.

The lack of motivation and energy, combined with discomfort when interacting with others, leads to increased isolation and feelings of extreme loneliness for SAD sufferers during the winter. Trying to get outside daily and maintain social connections can help minimize it.

The Difficulty of Concentrating and Coping with Stress

In the throes of a seasonal depressive episode, individuals with SAD often struggle significantly with concentration issues and feel overwhelmed by stress that previously seemed manageable.

Trouble Concentrating:

Mental fogginess and difficulty focusing are hallmark symptoms. The constant fatigue makes it hard to stay alert. Individuals may stare blankly, lose their train of thought mid-sentence, or take a long time recalling facts and words.

Difficulty Learning New Things:

Trying to learn something new feels exhausting. Retaining information gets tough when you are depressed and low on energy. Feelings of being mentally "dull" set in, like the mind is operating in slow motion.

Harder to Make Decisions:

With reduced mental clarity, even small daily decisions seem monumentally difficult. Those with SAD get paralyzed by analyzing options or avoiding making any decision altogether. Plans get put off or neglected.

More Distractible:

Attention easily drifts when you need more mental focus. Little noises, passing thoughts, and diversions prevent completing tasks. Starting projects drags on while finishing them seems impossible.

Overwhelmed Easily:

Any additional stimulus can feel like an overload when already carrying mental fatigue. Work assignments, family obligations, or changes in routine overwhelm depleted mental reserves. Coping with stress becomes extremely difficult.

Prone to Errors:

Concentration deficits lead to making more errors both at work and at home. Forgetting simple tasks, missing details, or misplacing items becomes common. It requires extra effort to be accurate.

The brain fog that sets in during seasonal depression takes an immense toll on productivity, performance, and the ability to manage life's daily demands. Routine responsibilities like work, errands, and childcare feel exhausting. Building in mental breaks and practicing stress-reduction techniques helps cope.

Suicide Risk and Importance of Treatment

Seasonal Affective Disorder (SAD) is a serious medical condition that requires professional treatment. If you or someone you know is experiencing suicidal thoughts or intentions, please reach out to the National Suicide

Prevention Lifeline at 1-800-273-8255 or a trusted mental health professional right away. There is help and hope available.

Seasonal Affective Disorder involves significant changes in mood, energy levels, and daily function that can severely impair quality of life during depressive episodes. Without effective treatment, SAD can recur every year as the seasons change. Some experience SAD symptoms even in the summer months. This persistent struggle can feel endless and hopeless.

However, it is crucial for anyone with SAD to understand two truths:

1. SAD is a clinically recognized disorder; it is not your fault or a personal weakness.
2. Effective treatments for SAD do exist; the condition is manageable.

While the depressive periods can be profoundly difficult, the key is recognizing SAD as the underlying cause rather than blaming yourself. View it as you would any other medical condition requiring treatment.

The good news is that SAD is highly treatable through psychotherapy, medications, light therapy, vitamin D, and lifestyle adjustments. Most people experience significant improvements within the first year of dedicated treatment.

With a customized treatment plan, periods of depression progressively shorten and feel less severe. Symptoms become easier to manage each year. Eventually, remission is possible for many individuals.

Do not lose hope if one particular treatment does not work well for you. It often takes some trial and error to find the best intervention for your individual needs. However, persevering is worth it.

The first step is talking to your doctor for a clinical evaluation and initial treatment recommendations. Ongoing counseling provides critical support. It also helps counteract the isolation that SAD can cause.

While SAD poses substantial challenges, the condition does not define you. Better days are ahead—your health, happiness, and comfort matter. If seasonal depression goes untreated, remember that help is available; you need to reach out for it.

Chapter 4

Treating SAD Medically

Types of Light Therapy and How to Use Them

Light therapy, also known as phototherapy, is considered the first-line treatment for SAD. It works by replacing the natural sunlight that is missing in winter. The light mimics outdoor light exposure to adjust circadian rhythms and brain chemicals linked to mood. Here are the main types:

Bright Light Therapy:

This uses a specialized lamp that emits up to 10,000 lux of white fluorescent light without UV rays. These lamps filter out harmful ultraviolet rays while producing a bright, full-spectrum light. Patients sit about 1 foot from the light for 30–60 minutes daily.

Dawn Simulation:

A dawn simulator is a device placed by the bed that gradually brightens to simulate a natural sunrise over 30–60 minutes. This can make morning awakenings easier for SAD patients with daytime drowsiness and sleep phase delays.

Light Therapy Lamps:

Portable light therapy boxes or lamps enable convenient at-home use. The lamp is placed on a table, and users sit near it for daily sessions. These lamps are also available as wake-up alarm clocks. Some provide both bright white light and simulated sunrise effects.

Light Therapy Visors:

These devices look like baseball caps with small light units embedded. They aim the light directly at the eyes to target light-sensitive receptors. Visors allow moving around during treatment. However, they may be less effective than stationary therapy with bright lamps.

Desk Lamps:

Special SAD therapy desk lamps are made to provide bright light exposure throughout the day. These help combat midday energy slumps and afternoon drowsiness. They can boost mood while working.

Light Therapy Glasses:

Some devices resemble sunglasses with small LED lights. They also deliver targeted light exposure by beaming it directly into the eyes. These offer convenience but may be less powerful.

Light therapy requires obtaining an appropriate high-intensity light source and using it regularly each morning during the darker months. Gazing directly at the light allows retinal receptors to transmit signals that lift mood, improve alertness, and regulate the body clock. Daily exposure for at least 30 minutes is recommended for the best results.

Antidepressants and Other Medications Used to Treat SAD

Along with light therapy, certain medications may be prescribed to help manage SAD, including:

Selective Serotonin Reuptake Inhibitors (SSRIs):

SSRIs like sertraline, fluoxetine, and citalopram are commonly prescribed. SSRIs prevent serotonin's reabsorption (reuptake), leaving more circulating to affect mood positively. They are taken daily.

Serotonin Norepinephrine Reuptake Inhibitors (SNRIs):

SNRIs such as venlafaxine and duloxetine also inhibit the reuptake of norepinephrine. This added effect can boost energy levels. Duloxetine may also reduce sensitivity to pain.

Bupropion:

This atypical antidepressant is a norepinephrine-dopamine reuptake inhibitor. Also, blocking dopamine reuptake may help improve focus, concentration, and motivation.

Mirtazapine:

Mirtazapine enhances serotonin and norepinephrine signaling. It specifically targets serotonin receptors, thought to play a role in seasonal mood changes. This medication commonly causes drowsiness.

Melatonin:

Some studies indicate melatonin may help resynchronize circadian rhythms disrupted in SAD. However, the results are mixed. Time-released doses before bedtime are suggested to avoid daytime drowsiness.

Light Therapy Adjuncts:

Certain medications, like fluoxetine, may enhance light therapy effects when used together by making the brain more responsive to light exposure. Discuss potential synergies with your prescriber.

Off-Label Medications:

Drugs approved for conditions like anxiety, ADD/ADHD, Parkinson's disease, and epilepsy may be prescribed off-label to manage SAD for some patients.

Of course, medications come with side effects, risks, and drug interactions. Working closely with your psychiatrist to determine effectiveness and adjust dosages is imperative. Maintenance therapy during vulnerable seasons may be recommended rather than year-round treatment. Finding the right medication or combination can significantly improve seasonal depression.

Vitamin D Supplements and Other Nutraceuticals

Vitamin D:

Also known as the "sunshine vitamin," vitamin D levels drop with less sun exposure. Correcting winter-time D deficiency may lift the seasonal mood. Oral supplements are effective; 800-4000 IU of D3 daily is typical. Get blood levels tested to monitor.

Omega-3 Fatty Acids:

Omega-3s found in fish oil and some plant sources have anti-inflammatory effects on the brain. Supplementing omega-3s may improve SAD symptoms, though study results are mixed. Try 1000–2000 mg of EPA and DHA omega-3s daily.

Vitamin B12:

B12 is important in energy metabolism and brain function. Low B12 is linked to depression. Supplements or B12-rich foods may combat fatigue. Get B12 levels checked before supplementing.

Folate:

Folate deficiency can also cause low mood and poor concentration. Correcting any folate deficiencies through diet or supplements of 400–800 mcg may lessen SAD symptoms.

Probiotics:

Emerging research shows gut-brain connections. Probiotic supplements may influence neurotransmitter production and decrease pro-inflammatory gut bacteria strains linked to depression.

Saffron:

Derived from the saffron crocus flower, this spice contains antioxidants that help with anxiety and depression. Try taking 30 mg twice daily.

5-HTP:

Made from the amino acid tryptophan, 5-HTP converts to serotonin in the brain. 100–300 mg daily potentially relieves SAD symptoms. Do not combine with antidepressants.

St. John's Wort:

This herbal supplement mildly inhibits serotonin and dopamine reuptake. Clinical trials demonstrate possible effectiveness for mild to moderate depression. Check for drug interactions.

Certain nutraceuticals and herbal supplements may help control SAD, particularly in milder cases, when used carefully under medical guidance. Adequate dosages taken consistently are the most beneficial. Note that the quality and purity of supplements vary widely. Consult your doctor.

When to Seek a Diagnosis and Treatment from Your Doctor

If you experience symptoms of sadness, fatigue, social withdrawal, sleep issues, appetite changes, and loss of pleasure or motivation that follow a seasonal pattern, make an appointment with your doctor right away to discuss the evaluation and treatment of a possible Seasonal Affective Disorder (SAD).

You should seek medical advice if you have seasonal depressive symptoms that:

- Cause significant distress and make it hard to function normally.
- Interfere with work performance, productivity, and concentration.
- Disrupt relationships and isolate yourself from family and friends.

- Persist daily for at least two weeks.
- Feel completely different from your normal mood and energy levels.
- Return predictably every year as the seasons change.

Even milder forms of seasonal depression warrant checking in with your physician to explore options. Do not write it off as "winter blues" if you consistently struggle when the weather turns cold.

It is important to get ahead of SAD and have treatment plans in place before it strikes hard. Make appointments to discuss options a few months before you typically start feeling depressed. For fall-winter SAD, plan ahead in early September.

Tracking your moods, energy levels, sleep patterns, and any other symptoms on a seasonal calendar can help identify patterns to share with your doctor. Consider any seasonal triggers you notice, like weather, light exposure, holidays, etc.

Come to your appointment prepared to explain how you feel during certain seasons compared to other times of the year. Be honest about the degree to which symptoms impair your daily life. Your doctor needs this information for an accurate clinical assessment.

If diagnosed with SAD, follow your doctor's recommendations diligently regarding light therapy, medications, supplements, psychotherapies, and lifestyle adjustments. Consistency is key, even when your mood starts improving. Do not wait until you feel terrible again to seek help; be proactive.

With your doctor's guidance, you can effectively manage seasonal depression. Taking charge of SAD gives you back control over your mood, activities, relationships, and happiness during the seasons ahead.

Chapter 5

Lifestyle Changes That Help SAD

Exercising Regularly for Mood Boosts

Exercise is a powerful way to alleviate the depression, fatigue, and lack of motivation associated with SAD. Working physical activity into your routine, especially in the colder months, provides multiple mental and physical health benefits:

1. **Boosts endorphins:** Exercise releases feel-good endorphins, the body's natural opioids that elevate mood and relieve stress. Endorphin surges help counteract the negative feelings of SAD.

2. **Increases energy:** Physical exertion can leave you feeling energized rather than drained. This helps combat the constant exhaustion of seasonal depression.

3. **Reduces anxiety:** Exercise decreases levels of the stress hormone cortisol. It also relaxes tense muscles, which can make anxiety worse.

4. **Improves sleep:** Regular exercise leads to deeper, higher-quality sleep at night. This can help reverse the disrupted sleep patterns of SAD.

5. **Supports circulation:** Exercise gets the blood and oxygen flowing, which may help the winter doldrums by improving circulation to the brain.

6. **Provides vitamin D:** If exercising outdoors, even short walks expose you to natural sunlight for vitamin D absorption through the skin.

7. **Encourages socializing:** Group classes and activities, jogging with a friend, or playing sports builds social connections. This helps avoid the isolation of SAD.

8. **Boosts self-esteem:** Meeting exercise goals cultivates a sense of accomplishment. Pride in your strength and fitness is an antidote to the feelings of worthlessness that SAD can cause.

Overall, committing to exercise 3-5 times per week for at least 30 minutes will go a long way toward maintaining mental and physical health during the winter. Even a short walk outdoors makes a difference. Find forms of exercise you enjoy and mix them up to increase motivation. Your improved mood and energy will motivate you to keep going.

Tailoring Your Diet to Help Alleviate SAD Symptoms

Dietary changes can make a significant difference in managing SAD. Focus on eating patterns that stabilize energy levels, improve mood, support gut health, and avoid trigger foods that exacerbate symptoms:

1. **Stabilize blood sugar:** Keep blood sugar balanced by eating small, frequent meals containing protein, fiber, and complex carbs. This prevents energy crashes and sugar cravings.

2. **Boost mood-friendly foods:** Increase serotonin-boosting foods like fatty fish, nuts, seeds, and leafy greens. Limit processed carbs and sugar, which cause crashes.

3. **Hydrate:** Dehydration exacerbates fatigue and moodiness. Sip water consistently throughout the

day. Herbal teas provide hydration without caffeine interference.

4. **Add probiotics:** Sauerkraut, kimchi, kefir, and yogurt contain probiotics to support gut-brain health. A daily probiotic supplement helps, too.

5. **Increase anti-inflammatory foods:** Consume more tomatoes, olive oil, nuts, fruits, veggies, and omega-3 fatty acids to control systemic depression-related inflammation.

6. **Get sunlight-derived nutrients:** Load up on vitamin D-rich foods and antioxidants in citrus fruits, berries, yellow and orange produce, and dark leafy greens.

7. **Watch alcohol intake:** Limit alcohol, which worsens depression. If drinking, opt for red wine in moderation due to resveratrol's antidepressant effects.

8. **Portion control:** Be cautious of overeating to cope with SAD. Get nutrients from quality whole foods rather than comfort junk foods.

9. **Eat consistently:** Depressive episodes can destroy appetite. Make yourself eat something small every few hours, even when unhungry.

10. **Discuss supplements:** Talk to your doctor about vitamin D, probiotics, omega-3 fatty acids, or other supplements that may be helpful.

Adjusting your eating patterns provides essential support alongside other SAD treatments. What you put in your body impacts how you feel physically and mentally, for better or worse.

Setting Up a Consistent Sleep Routine

Regular sleep and wake times can significantly relieve the fatigue, difficulty sleeping, and daytime drowsiness associated with SAD. Aim for consistency with the following sleep hygiene tips:

- Go to bed and wake up at the same time daily, even on weekends and holidays. This stabilizes your circadian clock.

- Develop a relaxing pre-bed routine, like reading or taking a bath. Cues signal your brain that it is time for sleep.

- Unwind and dim the lights a few hours before bed to increase natural melatonin release.

- Avoid screens, large meals, and vigorous activity for 1-2 hours before bedtime. These are stimulating.

- Make your sleep environment cool, quiet, dark, and comfortable. Block out all light sources and noise.

- Invest in supportive sleep aids like blackout curtains, eye masks, earplugs, and weighted blankets.

- If tossing and turning in bed for over 20 minutes, get up and do a calming activity until sleepy. Please do not force it.

- Limit napping to 30 minutes max, and avoid naps after 3 p.m. This prevents interference with nighttime sleep.

- Try meditation, relaxation exercises, or light yoga before bed to ease anxiety and quiet your mind.

- Expose yourself to bright light first thing in the morning to suppress melatonin and boost cortisol alertness.

- Exercise regularly, but not right before bed. Get moving earlier in the day for the best energy benefits.

With consistency, these habits will improve sleep quality and duration. Aim for 7-9 hours a night. Proper sleep makes handling SAD's ups and downs much more manageable.

The Importance of Social Interaction and Strong Support Systems

The social withdrawal and isolation of SAD can become a self-perpetuating cycle. Making an effort to interact with close family and friends regularly can make a profound difference in coping with the depressive period.

Schedule video chats or phone dates to catch up with long-distance loved ones. Hearing familiar voices counteracts loneliness, even from afar. Send care packages or handwritten letters to maintain bonds.

For local relatives and friends, mark weekly in-person visits on your calendar. Follow through on these commitments even when you do not feel up to it. Social mood boosts will follow.

Join friends for short walks outdoors on sunny days. Sunlight exposure and fresh air lifts mood, while socializing adds accountability for staying active.

Share your SAD experiences and treatment plans with loved ones so they understand the changes in your mood and energy. Their support will strengthen your resolve.

If you feel reluctant to see people when depressed, ask a close friend to encourage you not to isolate gently. They can persuade you to take part in an activity.

Pursue hobbies like crafting, book clubs, or art in group settings. Shared interests nurture meaningful connections and provide a sense of fulfillment.

Consider adopting a pet for daily companionship and responsibility. Caring for a pet boosts oxytocin, serotonin, and dopamine. Their unconditional love is medicinal.

Seek talk therapy or join a support group to discuss seasonal depression challenges with others who can empathize. You are not alone.

Prioritizing genuine social bonds provides a buffer against the isolation of SAD. People give you a lifeline to hold onto during the long winter months ahead. Reach out and let them lift you up.

Indoor Hobbies and Activities to Embrace During the Winter

It is tempting to go into hibernation mode when SAD strikes in the winter, but engaging in enjoyable indoor activities can boost your spirits. Consider these options:

1. ***Read novels, magazines, and poetry.*** Curling up under a blanket with a gripping book provides a cozy retreat. Reading transports your mind.

2. ***Do arts, crafts, and DIY projects.*** Drawing, knitting, woodworking, and scrapbooking tap into your creativity. Making things feels empowering.

3. ***Play board games and puzzles.*** Sharing laughter and friendly competition keeps your mind sharp. Puzzles provide absorbing focus.

4. ***Listen to or play uplifting music.*** Make playlists of your favorite feel-good songs. Learning an instrument channels energy.

5. ***Watch funny movies and shows.*** Laughter truly is therapeutic medicine. Have a comedy marathon or movie night.

6. ***Write in a journal.*** Jot thoughts, hopes, and dreams. Review past entries to see if you have overcome previous winters.

7. ***Take online courses.*** Learn new skills and topics. Give your brain a workout with virtual lectures.

8. ***Do indoor exercise.*** Gym equipment, workout videos, and yoga mats enable home workouts. Alternatively, dance around while cleaning!

9. ***Pursue your passions.*** Sewing, photography, baking, and painting—dive into meaningful hobbies that make you lose track of time.
10. ***Play with pets.*** Furry friends provide endless entertainment. Engage pets with playtime and cuddles.

In winter, switching to cozy clothes and socks to get comfy while engaging in favorite indoor activities can make the season feel special rather than isolating. Build a routine, alternating between productive tasks and fun leisure time. Before you know it, spring will come again.

Chapter 6

Mental Strategies for Coping with SAD

Identifying and Reframing Negative Thoughts

The sad, anxious thoughts that accompany SAD can deeply impact our outlook. Learning to identify negative thought patterns and reframe them in a more positive light takes practice but can improve mood.

Pinpoint automatic negative thoughts. These pop up involuntarily and seem believable at the moment. Examples: *"I am worthless. I will never get better. Winter will last forever."*

Journal about your thoughts. Writing them down increases self-awareness and examines truth more objectively. Are they overly dramatic or irrational?

Collect evidence against the thoughts. This weakens their power. List past examples of accomplishments, recovery, or enjoyment despite SAD.

Generate alternative thoughts. Come up with more balanced, helpful responses to counter the negative thinking. *"This winter will not last forever. I can get through this."*

Imagine advising a loved one. We are often kinder to others. What advice would you give a struggling friend? Treat yourself with that same compassion.

Focus on each day rather than looking far ahead. Reframe thoughts to stay in the present moment: *"I am going to take it one day at a time and find moments of joy."*

Consider the thought's purpose. Sometimes, we ruminate, trying to gain control. Reframe to accept things beyond your control. Let it go.

Revisit your thoughts once your mood improves. Were they rational at the time? Please do not beat yourself up; it is SAD distorting your thinking.

Over time, regularly reframing pessimistic thoughts in a more balanced way can improve your outlook, even when SAD is severe. Be patient, and keep practicing.

Practicing Mindfulness and Living in the Present Moment

Mindfulness involves increasing awareness of the present moment with openness, curiosity, and non-judgment. Practicing mindfulness techniques can reduce rumination about the past and worrying about the future, which exacerbates SAD. Try these tips:

1. ***Observe sensations.*** Note the physical feelings, sights, sounds, and smells around you. Getting out of your head reduces overthinking.
2. ***Describe surroundings.*** Mentally describe details of your environment without judging or analyzing. Keep returning your focus outward.
3. ***Focus on your breath.*** When your mind wanders, gently redirect attention to the sensations of breathing in and out.

4. ***Let your thoughts come and go.*** Thoughts will arise. Do not suppress them. Notice them, then refocus on the present without following thought trains.

5. ***Stay calm in the chaos.*** When feeling stressed or overwhelmed, pause and observe the anxiety without reacting. Breathe through it.

6. ***Do a body scan.*** Slowly notice any tension or relaxation in each part of your body, from head to toe. Release clenched muscles.

7. ***Go on autopilot less.*** Engage your senses fully when eating, walking, washing dishes, or brushing your teeth. Appreciate the mundane.

8. ***Find joy in small moments.*** Savor your morning coffee, sunlight through the window, kids laughing, and your favorite song. Even when sad, there is beauty.

9. ***Be gentle with yourself.*** Do not criticize yourself for "doing it wrong." Mindfulness is the process of continually returning focus to the present.

The benefits compound over time. With daily practice, mindfulness shifts perspective, reducing the tendency to fixate on negative thoughts. You gain control over SAD.

Maintaining the Perspective that SAD is Temporary

When engulfed in the daily struggles of SAD, it is easy to catastrophize and feel like the depression, exhaustion, and isolation will last indefinitely. Maintaining the perspective that SAD symptoms are temporary can help preserve hope. Consider these outlook adjustments:

1. ***Remember previous years.*** Look back at past winters, where the seasons changed, your mood lifted, and you felt like yourself again. This, too, shall pass.

2. ***Focus on getting through it one day at a time.*** Do not expect an immediate cure. Making incremental progress is still moving forward. Small goals are more manageable.

3. ***Recall that brighter days are coming.*** Winter only lasts several months, and spring reliably returns with its warming sunlight and awakening nature. This difficult period will expire.

4. ***Know that there will be ups and downs.*** SAD often ebbs and flows throughout the season. Bad days are followed by better days. Mood fluctuations are normal this time of year.

5. ***Do not compare your experience to others.*** We all have different seasonal responses. Your SAD journey is unique to you. Only compare to your past seasons.

6. ***Expect setbacks occasionally.*** Having a horrible day does not negate all your progress. It is just part of the nonlinear path to managing SAD long-term.

7. ***Look for small reprieves.*** A funny movie, a friend's visit, a sunny afternoon walk—savor brief mood boosts while they last.

8. ***Remind yourself, "This too shall pass."*** The winter months ahead will pass. Spring blossoms will emerge again. This down period helps you appreciate the ups.

9. ***Keep pursuing treatment.*** Do not lose hope that you will find an effective approach to controlling your symptoms. It takes trial and error.

With seasonal depression, maintaining perspective regarding the temporary nature of symptoms can help you ride out difficult periods. The forecast ahead predicts brighter days returning soon.

Focusing on Your Power to Choose Your Reaction

SAD can make you feel powerless against seasonal changes, dragging your mood down. However, even in the depths of depression, you have control over one thing: your reaction. Consciously focusing on your power to choose your response can be comforting and liberating.

1. ***Release the notion that you can control the seasons.*** Accept that light changes are outside your control. Do not fight the weather or beat yourself up over symptoms.

2. ***Realize you have authority over your actions.*** How you choose to respond remains your choice. Take back a sense of agency.

3. ***Own your feelings.*** You cannot dictate emotions, but you can decide how much to engage with them. Do not let them own you.

4. ***Focus on facts rather than interpretations.*** "It is cloudy today" is a factual thought. "This gloomy day proves winter will never end" is an unhelpful interpretation. Stick to the facts.

5. ***Reframe your experiences as opportunities.*** A difficult day could be viewed as a frustrating

setback or a chance to practice resilience. Reframing empowers.

6. ***Consider the benefits.*** The winter weather encourages coziness and hygge. Shorter days provide an excuse to sleep in and curl up indoors. Do more than just see the negatives.

7. ***List small, daily choices.*** What to wear, eat, watch, and listen to—focus on little choices within your control. Small actions empower us, too.

8. ***Set mini-goals.*** Choosing to start one new self-care habit this week or take one daily walk gives you a sense of forward motion.

9. ***Remind yourself, "I can choose my response."*** Become aware when you are on autopilot and reacting. Check in with what you want to choose at that moment.

The seasons may change, but your ability to consciously respond remains. Even on the darkest days, you can find pockets of choice and control through self-awareness.

Chapter 7

Making Your Environment SAD-Proof

Maximizing Natural Light Through Environmental Design

Exposure to plentiful natural light, especially in the morning, is key to managing SAD. Optimizing the light in your home and workspace through strategic design choices can make a significant difference. Consider these tips:

1. ***Position work and living spaces on the east.*** Morning sun exposure is ideal. East-facing rooms get flooded with sunny morning light to help regulate the body's clock.

2. ***Open the blinds and curtains fully.*** As soon as you wake up, open all window coverings to let in every bit of morning sun. Keep them open all day to maximize the light.

3. ***Move furniture near windows.*** Sitting right beside windows at work and home ensures you receive the most light exposure throughout the day.

4. ***Install skylights or solar tubes.*** Adding skylights to rooms lacking windows or installing solar light tubes helps bring brightness. Keep them dust-free.

5. ***Choose sheer curtains.*** Select breezy, sheer white curtains to filter glare but allow light flow. They scatter light gently across rooms.

6. ***Add mirrors and reflective surfaces.*** Mirrors and polished metal surfaces bounce and amplify existing light naturally. Strategically place them to make rooms brighter.

7. ***Paint walls with light colors.*** White or light yellow walls prevent light absorption and make spaces brighter. Gloss or semi-gloss finishes also reflect light well.

8. ***Use glass room dividers.*** Opt for glass partitions or interior windows rather than solid walls. This allows light to pass through adjacent spaces.

9. ***Trim window obstructions.*** Cut back outdoor trees, bushes, vines, or structures that obscure windows year-round and limit light entry.
10. ***Keep the lights on during daylight.*** Please do not turn off overhead lights in winter since their illumination supplements natural light nicely.

With some strategic rearranging and design adjustments, you can maximize every bit of precious natural light in your spaces during the darker months.

Adding Artificially Bright Light at Home and Work

While maximizing natural sunlight exposure should take priority, adding sources of artificially bright light can also help compensate for gloomy days and short winter hours.

Install bright white LED light bulbs at home in frequently used lamps and fixtures. Choose bulbs rated at least 5000K to simulate natural daylight. Avoid soft white bulbs.

Position floor and table lamps in the corners of rooms to distribute light widely throughout the space. Bouncing light off walls reaches more areas.

Use timers or smart bulbs to automatically turn lights on in the morning to support your circadian rhythm. Slowly increasing light intensity mimics the sunrise.

Invest in a sunrise alarm clock that brightens gradually. The light rouses you naturally while triggering hormones that increase alertness.

Obtain a light therapy box designed specifically to treat SAD using 10000 lux white light. Sit near it for 30+ minutes daily.

Try a wearable light therapy visor if consistent sitting is difficult. It beams light directly at your eyes. Use it during activities or chores.

At work, personal bright light therapy lamps are excellent for desk use. Position the light off to the side at eye level as you work.

Install full-spectrum daylight bulbs in overhead office lighting and task lamps. The brighter light keeps afternoon energy levels up.

Step outside periodically throughout the workday. Even a short walk absorbs some natural light.

Use an app like F.lux on computers that filters out blue light. The warmer hues are less stimulating in the evenings.

Avoid total darkness in the evenings to support the circadian rhythm. Keep a low-level lamp on rather than turning the lights off.

Adding bright, full-spectrum light sources throughout your home and workplace helps compensate for the dark, dismal weather outside. Consult your doctor about using phototherapy devices safely and effectively.

Keeping Spaces Decluttered and Soothing to Support Mental Health

The state of your surroundings impacts your inner state of mind. Keeping indoor spaces clean, decluttered, and soothingly arranged can aid relaxation and reduce stress when struggling with SAD:

1. ***Declutter often.*** Remove clutter and things you no longer use or need. Excess stuff is visually distracting and mentally draining. Simplify your environment.

2. ***Establish convenient homes for items.*** Give everything a designated spot to live. Staying

organized prevents losing important things in a messy pile.

3. ***Do regular cleanings.*** Dust, vacuum, and tidy routinely. Fresh, clean spaces feel uplifting versus dirty, cluttered ones, which breed anxiety.

4. ***Open up rooms.*** Remove furniture obstructing pathways and natural light. Free flow improves mood and circulation.

5. ***Incorporate nature.*** The artwork's houseplants, flowers, and garden scenes purify the air and connect you to nature when you cannot be outdoors.

6. ***Use cozy textiles.*** Soft blankets, plush rugs, and curtains create snuggly spaces that comfort and soothe.

7. ***Play soothing music.*** Curate playlists of tranquil instrumental or nature sounds to relax and unwind.

8. ***Diffuse calming scents.*** Lavender, eucalyptus, and chamomile aromas are calming. Alternatively, simmer cinnamon sticks and citrus peels.

9. ***Display positive affirmations.*** Frame inspiring quotes, notes, and photos of happier times as uplifting reminders.

10. ***Pick restful colors.*** Paint walls or add accent pieces in serene blues, greens, and neutrals that ease the mind.

Edit your environment to eliminate chaos and introduce elements of relaxation. Your surroundings can help instill inner calm or exacerbate stress. Make choices that prime your spaces for peace as you navigate SAD.

The Importance of Planning Regular Outdoor Time Year-Round to Cope with SAD

While the colder, darker months make going outside unappealing when you have SAD, getting a daily dose of fresh air and sunlight can significantly brighten your mood. Planning outdoor time into each day should be a priority.

1. ***Get sunlight first thing in the morning.*** Just 10-15 minutes outdoors right after waking up can help reset your body clock and boost vitamin D absorption.

2. ***Schedule outdoor breaks at work.*** Even a 10-minute walk outdoors on your lunch break or between meetings boosts your mood.

3. ***Do activities outdoors rather than indoors whenever possible.*** Take phone calls, read, or eat

meals outside to multi-task self-care with daily obligations.

4. ***Socialize outside.*** Meet friends for a walk, back patio hangout, or picnic at a park to combine social interaction with light exposure.

5. ***Soak up sunlight on weekends.*** Make outdoor plans each Saturday and Sunday, like hiking, winter sports, running errands, or yard work. Avoid staying indoors all day.

6. ***Plan winter travel to sunnier climates.*** When you return, a few days of vacationing somewhere warm and bright provides a big mood reset.

7. ***Time outdoors around weather patterns.*** Check the forecast for sunny days after storms roll through. Maximize time outside during brighter spells.

8. ***Bundle up in layers.*** Do not let cold and snow deter outdoor excursions. Wear warm boots, a thick coat, gloves, a hat, and a scarf; embrace the weather.

9. ***Try a portable UV lamp.*** If the weather prohibits outdoor time, sit beside an artificial sunlight lamp indoors for 30 minutes for similar benefits.

10. ***Pick active winter hobbies.*** Shoveling snow, skiing, ice skating, and snowshoeing provide exercise outdoors. Moving your body warms you naturally.